A Time Remembered

Girlhood memories of the 1930's and 40's

Marjorie Major

ISBN: 978-1-326-23323-5

PublishNation, London
www.publishnation.co.uk

Contents

Christmas

'Has he been?' I cried as I was startled into consciousness in the half-light of early morning by my older sisters' exclamations of delight.

'Yes', they chorused and I groped in the semi-darkness for my Christmas stocking – one of father's socks which I had hung on the brass knob of the single iron bedstead in which I slept. I was overjoyed to discover it had been filled for I had been afraid Father Christmas would not come to me. Mother had told me he might not if I continued to be so naughty.

My little friend Gerald Richardson – who lived next door – and I had been found playing in the wash-house turning the wheel of the large wringing machine, or mangle. We had already flattened two unsuspecting worms we had found on the garden path and were about to start on another when we were discovered. We were five years old and were dealt with severely. At that age we were expected to behave in a reasonable manner instead of which we appeared to be showing signs of criminal tendencies having the day before pulled the bung out of the rain barrel. The drain being blocked with winter debris, the flood went undiscovered, until Father, coming home from work in the dark, wheeled his bicycle into the yard and got his feet wet. Gerald and I were duly walloped by our respective mothers, mine being very firm on the subject of Father Christmas not visiting naughty children.

All must have been forgiven me, for here it was Christmas Day and I had been visited! The contents of the stocking varied little down the years. Inside the toe there was always an apple, orange, nuts – still in their shells of course – to be eaten later when I could grab a turn with the nut-crackers, some toffees, jelly babies, liquorice root, which tasted pretty foul, but we always ate it when really hungry, a packet of coloured crayons, a colouring book, plasticine and maybe a card game such as Happy Families or Snap and tiny ball game puzzles. We young ones received a bright new penny and occasionally chocolate ones. My favourite toy was the snake which whistled and shot out in a long wriggly movement when you blew it. How we enjoyed making the adults jump with this toy. This Christmas morning beside my bed stood a doll's tiny push chair with the cutest little black topsy doll sitting in it ..... My joy was complete!

There were six of us children. The oldest Edith was thirteen years old, Eva, a year and a day younger. Jack came next at nine, then Bernard who was six and a half, just eighteen months older than me. Baby Robert was just a few months old and Harry was not yet born. Mother certainly had her hands full.

We lived in a large old house situated within walking distance of the town docks. It had five bedrooms and an attic in which we younger children used to play when the weather was too bad to play outside. This attic had cupboards built all round the eaves. They were very low and you could crawl inside straight from the floor. I recall being fastened in one of these cupboards by my brothers in some game. It was very dark and I became rather frightened, particularly when they went off and forgot about me. I was hysterical by the time I was finally rescued and to this day I suffer from slight claustrophobia. Thank you my dear brothers!

On the kitchen wall of the house were a row of bells. A board beneath showed the names of the rooms to which the maid servants could be summoned. We had no maid, only Mrs Mallory, a terrifying hoarse-voiced old Scots woman who came on wash days and when Mother was ill or confined with the latest arrival.

Mrs Mallory used to say we children were over indulged and when in charge of us would ration us according to age. I remember complaining bitterly to my mother who was in bed, half delirious at the time with double pneumonia and pleurisy, that I was half starved having been sent to school on a horrible watery bowl of porridge and half a slice of toast. Being the fifth child and thin and wiry with an appetite like a horse, I really suffered under Mrs Mallory's regime. Mother told us many years later that the poor woman had several children of her own to support and a drunken husband, so there was some reason for her thinking we were dreadfully spoiled.

This Christmas I remember vividly, mainly because of receiving the black doll, something I had longed for, and also because of the Christmas party to which we were invited at our paternal grandparent's house.

After attending mass at St. Wilfred's church we were thrilled to find it had been snowing. We trudged home and divesting ourselves of our best coats rushed out into the yard to build a snowman and to have a snowball fight.

Before dinner came the giving of presents to each other. Being so young I don't remember giving any myself on that occasion but in later years I do. No matter how small the present it had to be wrapped up in lots of newspaper to make a sizable parcel, which we then tied with coloured thread – we raided mother's sewing box for this – the recipient's name tag would be made from an old Christmas card. All the parcels were put in mother's large wash basket and we all enjoyed opening them up.

We were poor by today's standards. We got only one penny pocket money on a Saturday and whilst Grandfather Dickenson lived with us we had a Friday penny from him. We earned extra by running errands for neighbours and collecting empty jam jars, returning them to the corner shop. Shopkeepers would give a half-penny for a 2lb jar and a farthing for a 1lb jar.

My parents' never went into public houses but father liked a glass of Guinness at the week-end and a Corona cigar. Sometimes we had lemonade out of bottles which had a glass marble in the neck, occasionally when I was older I would get the chance to return these

3

bottles. There was always a penny to be earned by doing so. It was still quite an effort to save enough to buy eight presents.

I invariably bought a packet of Kirby hair grips which cost one penny and cut it in half as presents for my two older sisters. I would buy bulls-eyes for the boys – their favourite sweet. They were enormous round balls which changed colour as one sucked them. They were sticky to handle as one was constantly removing them from one's mouth to see their colour. They were eventually taken off the market after several children choked to death on them.

Preparing for Christmas seemed to take ages. About six weeks before the event mother would announce that the following Saturday we would make the puddings and mincemeat. She always made four large puddings, one for Christmas dinner the others for special occasions throughout the coming year.

We willing helpers would stone the raisins – no seedless ones in those days. We would soak and skin the almonds, wash the currants and scrape the carrots to be grated into the pudding and the mincemeat. We would peel the apples and grate fresh orange and lemon peel. We also chopped the large pieces of suet into small particles and then put the lot through the mincing machine which was screwed into the white deal table that was mother's baking and cooking area, as well as our dining table.

When all the stirring was done – we each had a turn at this, in order to make our secret wish – we were then allowed to scrape the bowls clean. I regret to say we always squabbled about this, though mother would try and instil into us some sense of fair-play, my brothers always seemed to get more than their fair share. Because of the quantities involved mother always used the two large wash-stand basins, thoroughly scrubbed of course.

Father had put a bathroom into this house by converting the smallest bedroom so that we seldom washed in the wash-stand basin, but still they remained as part of the bedroom furnishings. Mostly we washed at the kitchen sink especially in the winter. Mother would line us up afterwards to inspect ears and hands. My brother Jack was always sent back to wash his ears and neck again. Mother used to say he only had a nodding acquaintance with soap and water.

After school about two weeks before the BIG DAY, we concentrated on making the Christmas decorations. Elbow deep in flour and water paste we would soldier on until our coloured paper chains stretched across every room.

We always had lots of balloons. I guess they must have been fairly cheap to buy. We had to use our own puff to blow them up – no such things as pumps in those days. It was very much a do-it-yourself era but we were never bored.

Mother had the best cure for any child who complained of having nothing to do. A job around the house could always be found, from cleaning father's Sunday boots to breaking up the block salt and rolling it into smoothness with a rolling pin.

'The devil finds work for idle hands', mother would say, quite unconscious of the humour in this remark, she would direct us to do so and so …. We soon learnt to busy ourselves at our own play.

So it was, on this Christmas Day, when I was five years old, that we finally sat down to our Christmas dinner. We always had a goose, turkeys being mainly American fare in those days. The practice of popping silver three-penny pieces – or bits as we called them – into the pudding caused lots of fun. It did ensure that we chewed every mouthful!

By three o'clock dinner was over and the dishes were put away. We were all dressed in our new clothes. I had on my new red jumper and navy pleated skirt. Every Christmas, as well as one major toy each, we always had something new to wear.

We trudged through the snow down the length of Lister Street. We lived at number twelve, our paternal grandparents Pank, at number seventy-three.

On entering the hall I remember being quite startled by the brightness, for Grandpa had gone 'all electric'. We still had gas lighting and the flickering flame of the fragile gas mantle and its glass globe, causing shadows in corners, seemed dim by comparison. This marvellous electric light was brilliant and the tall Christmas tree in the drawing room had pretty coloured lights all over it. The tree reached almost to the ceiling and was beautifully decorated with tinsel and coloured baubles. I saw a huge bunch of red cherries and some purple grapes made of shiny glass, amongst which were glittering birds with real feathers in their tails. Frosted snowballs and icicles of glass hung from every branch. I stood transfixed.

The assembled crowd were all father's family. They were gregarious people, constantly visiting each other. They were all from Tyne-side, South Shields. Grandfather had come to live in Hull some years before due to his work – he was shop manager of an engineering ship building firm, C.D. Holmes & Co. My father worked for the same firm as an iron moulder.

At this Christmas party was father's sister Belle, who together with her husband, Herbert Hudson and their two sons, Harry and Herbert, had recently returned from America. They had emigrated some years before but had not settled so returned to the U.K. They were currently staying with Grandma.

My cousin Harry was exactly one year younger than me. We shared the same birthday. I think I was seven before I stopped informing people that we were twins.

Opposite our house in Lister Street stood the Danish Embassy; it was an imposing building with a large garden and several steps leading up to the double front doors. We children called it the foreign house. Harry and I occasionally sat on the top step and peered into the garden over the brick wall. We sometimes saw people walking and talking together, we could never understand what they were saying.

One day a coach full of foreigners arrived. One lady who spoke English stopped to talk with us. I remember how astonished she looked when I told her Harry and I were twins, he being so fair haired and I so dark!

Aunt Eva, one of father's sisters was there that Christmas. She and her husband Rupert Hazell had come up from London for the festivities. They were professional entertainers.

Aunt had a beautiful soprano voice and had already made a name for herself at the Adelphi theatre in London and on concert platforms. She had been a pupil of the famous concert producer Miss Rowe and was a protégé of Lady Norah Bentick.

Uncle Rupert wrote his own songs and had many successes writing for George Robey and other famous people. He had made a hit in "Joy Bells" at the London Hippodrome some years before. He stayed on for the next Hippodrome triumph "Jig Saw" and afterwards appeared in "Pins and Needles" when it was produced in New York. He also appeared at the last Royal Performance at the London Coliseum, and got the first laugh of the evening according to the London Evening News.

A very versatile man, comedian, song writer, musician, Rupert also played the one-string fiddle as part of the act. As a lyric writer he had scores of well-known songs to his credit, 'See What I mean', 'Why of course', 'No, no', 'You'd be surprised' and 'Mrs Mephistopheles'. They both appeared in the Wylie Tate production at the Grand Pavilion in Bridlington in the late twenties. My aunt was only nineteen at the time and was billed as Eva Park. When she entered the variety theatre she took the stage name Elsie Day. Shortly before my aunt and uncle married they went on a world tour with Harry Lauder's company. Aunt caused rather a scandal in the family, and in the church we attended by marrying Rupert, for he was a divorced man, and the Roman Catholic Church did not recognise divorce. In later years I was to admire her stand very much. This talented pair often broadcast on the BBC and took part in the famous Itma show with Tommy Handley, Rupert again writing some of the script.

7

I vaguely remember being put to bed in grandma's large double bed and then much later waking up to find myself being carried home, looking up at the night sky with wonder at the brilliance of the stars. I have a theory that the things one sees for the first time are etched indelibly on the mind. I can visualise that sky and my first glimpse of it even now.

So ended that Christmas, subsequent ones were spent in similar vein except that this was the last gathering at grandma's house, she died the following year. I remember us children having to walk round the coffin in the drawing room. She lay white and still. She held a beautiful lily. How cold the brow which I was lifted up to kiss. I remember shrinking back for she didn't seem like grandma at all.

Only a short time before she had been laughing and playing with us in the field behind the summer bungalow grandpa owned, down Waxholme Road in Withernsea. This was where my brother Bernard and I had stayed for a holiday with our cousins. Grandma believed in feeding us well. I was too thin she said. If any of us declared ourselves to be full up with no room for pudding, she would line us up against the wall and have us bang our bottoms twenty-five times so as to make room for it.

I remember her smiling face as she helped me to make daisy chains and her teasing tickling under my chin with the butter-cups to see if I liked butter. I always did! Grandma's memory for me was synonymous with good food and laughter.

My parents gave a party every Christmas night. All would gather round the piano for a good bit of community singing. Mother was a classical pianist and at one time – before she married – had many pupils. She had a very good ear. You only had to hum a tune for her to play it. She knew all the popular songs of the day.

At one time she played the church organ. She was invited to play at Marton parish church when members of the Constable family who lived at Burton Constable Hall were married. Aunt Lillian was the soloist. I believe this came about through grandpa who, being friendly with the parish priest, used to take him in his Wolsey motor car to the hall each Saturday evening to play cards.

Some of the games we had at our parties were extraordinarily complicated. Someone would start with, 'I packed my case for India and in it I have one box of Doctor Procter's pink pills for pale people'. The next player would repeat this, adding whatever tongue twister he or she favoured.

The ones I remember were 'Two toads totally tired trying to trot to Tidbury', 'Three fat fishermen fishing for Friday', 'Four tinkling tinkermen tinkling tins', 'Five fat friars frying fish', 'Six sickly salmon slowly swimming' and many more. In fact up to as many players in the game. If anyone failed to remember a tongue twister a forfeit had to be paid. This usually took the form of a song or a monologue or a poem.

My uncles sang comic songs. Uncle Herbert, thin, sandy-haired – a jokey master butcher, manager of the Co-op shop – would sing, 'How does it feel to marry your ideal? Ever so goosey, goosey, goosey, goosey, Walking down the aisle in a kind of daze. Do you get the breeze up when the organ plays? How does it feel etc.' We would all join in the chorus.

Uncle Harry, a tall dark laconic engineer, would sing the Chinaman's song. 'In China town there lived a man his name was Chickeracka chi chi chan. His legs were long and his feet too small and this Chinaman couldn't walk at all.' The chorus was all gibberish really but for a long time I thought we were singing in the Chinese language.

Uncle Rupert's song was a firm favourite, we kids loved it. It was all about a ship-wreck. 'All the crew were in despair, some rushed here and some rushed there, but the Captain sat in the captain's chair and he played his ukulele as the ship went down.' There were about ten verses and at one time we knew them all.

Aunt Helen taught elocution and would recite dramatic poems. My favourite was 'Lorraine Loree', all about a young mother killed by falling off a horse whilst riding in a race she had been compelled to ride in by a cruel husband. I wept many a quiet tear over the last line. 'And no one but the baby cried for poor Lorraine Loree'.

At other more adult parties, after the young ones had been put to bed, more serious music would be played and sung. Mother would play Chopin waltzes and Rachmaninov's concerto's and Mendelsohn's Rustles of Spring. Aunts would sing duets.

We older children would be encouraged to show off our party pieces. My older sisters could sing very well and I was learning the piano, Bluebells of Scotland in variations and the Minute Waltz, etc. We were all encouraged to perform something. In more light-hearted vein brother Bernard would play the bones, mother would play 'Blaze Away' very fast on the piano and he would keep the rhythm going.

Father had a very good light tenor voice and with coaxing from mother would sing 'Thora' and 'Come into the garden Maud'. Our favourite though was the Bluebeard ballad.

This was a gory tale of a young maiden who married Baron Bluebeard and went to live in his castle. There was one room at the top which her husband forbade her to enter. One day he forgot to take the silver key of the door to this room with him. His young bride espied it and was tempted to open the door. She cried out in horror at the sight that met her eyes.

'Oh, mercy me', sang father, assuming a falsetto voice, 'What's this I see? I see them hanging on the wall'.

All the heads of Bluebeards former brides were hanging there. Too late to descend the stair, her husband catching her unaware is about to decapitate her when her brothers three come galloping into the courtyard to rescue her. How we all cheered at the end as Bluebeard met his doom. I believe this ballad was based on a true story of a French nobleman who murdered seven wives.

This was the pattern for most Christmas's until, when I was fourteen years old, World War Two began. Families became scattered and the world less secure.

The Secret

I stood on a crack and started to cry. 'What's the matter now?' asked my big sister Edith impatiently.

'I stood on a crack', I wailed, the tears starting.

'It's only a game, you silly! Our Mam's back is not going to break just 'cos you stood on a crack', said Edith, who was thirteen and knew most of the answers to my queries.

'Are you sure?' I said uncertainly.

'Yes, now come on or we'll be late for school again'. She took my hand and started to run.

Our school was a long way from our home. It took us twenty minutes to get there, even though we took a short-cut through Villa Place school play-ground when the gates were open. If anyone was late they would find the gates closed and would be made later still by having to go the long way round.

We were Catholics and attended St. Joseph's Convent school. I often wished I was going to Villa Place as it was so much nearer.

'I'm tired of running', I declared at last.

'Oh, come on it's not much further', Edith said.

I dragged my feet. 'I hate school and I don't want to go.'

'Well, hate it or not we all have to go', replied Edith. 'You'll get used to it the same as me. I've been going years longer than you, since before you were born. You will get to like it, honestly. Tell you what', she went on, 'you hurry up now and I promise to show you a big surprise at dinner time.'

'What is it?'

'Can't tell can I. It wouldn't be a surprise if I did.'

'Is it a secret then?'

'Yes if you like. Come on now hurry up.' We ran the rest of the way and arrived just as the bell stopped ringing.

My first teacher was a plump motherly nun who rejoiced in the name of Sister Mary Agnes. Our classroom was part of the convent and had a huge fireplace with a large guard in front. Brass corners on the guard gleamed in the glow of the fire which was always lit in winter time. If our feet were wet on arrival at school our socks would be hung on the guard to dry. There was a slipper box full of hand knitted slippers for us to wear. The nuns thought of everything and soon we were snug and warm again.

I remember my first geography lesson. We each had a book. It was purple with a picture of a long-necked animal on the front. We learned that this was a giraffe. Inside were pictures of other strange looking animals from all over the world. I had seen nothing like them before. This was long before television and visits to the cinema were rare. So my learning began, and I was interested. Dinner time soon came round and Edith was waiting for me by the school gate.

'What about the secret surprise'? I asked.

'Alright', she said 'but we'll have to hurry 'cos it's out of our way, and if it's not there you haven't to cry. It's not always there', she added obscurely.

'Why not'?

'It depends on the sun', she replied. Refusing to answer any more questions she hurried me along. Soon I grew tired and she gave me a pick-a-back. We arrived at our destination at last.

'Shut your eyes', she commanded, 'and don't open them until I tell you'. Then taking my hand she led me a little further down the street. 'Now!' said Edith.

I opened my eyes and found myself facing a wrought iron gate. 'Is that it'? I wondered. Then lifting my head I peered over the top of the gate. There, near the front door, was a large bird-cage on a stand.

The bird on the perch was just beautiful. The feathers on its chest were snowy white; its face was yellow with a brilliant orange spot at either side. The feathers on its back and wings were pale silvery grey and its tail was black and yellow and very long. Best of all though was a brilliant orange coxcomb which made the bird appear to be wearing a crown.

We stood there spellbound, gazing our fill. Suddenly, as a man with a spade in his hand came down the path the bird said, 'Wotcha matey'. I was mesmerised, the bird had spoken!

The man laughed in a kindly way and asked, 'Have you ever seen a bird like this before'? I shook my head. Edith said she had seen this one and had brought me along to see it. 'Well', the man said, 'I often put Sammy out here, he enjoys a bit of sunshine. He was born in New Zealand which is a very hot country y'know'.

'Is that what it is then - a Sammy'? I asked shyly.

Edith and the man laughed. 'Why bless you no, that's his name. This here is a cockatoo', he said.

My sister thanked the man for letting us see Sammy. 'Anytime your passing, stop and say hello', he replied, 'but don't go telling all your friends, too much attention over excites Sammy, see'!

'Shall we keep it a secret'? I asked.

'Aye do that', chuckled the man.

Edith took my hand. 'Goodbye', she said.

I walked home in a dream. When we got there I asked, 'Can we go and see Sammy tomorrow'?

'I'll see, it all depends on whether you can keep a secret, 'cos if you tell it won't be our secret any longer'.

'Oh, I won't tell, I won't', I cried. And at the time I meant it!

A Momentous Day

I was dressed in a new white dress with a blue satin sash and on my head was a tiny veil held there by a wreath of artificial flowers. Told to stand quite still for what seemed an inordinately long time, I had my picture taken. The occasion was my first communion when, along with the rest of the communicate class, I was to attend a special service at St. Wilfred's church in Hull.

Father took ages over photographing me and I was impatient to escape to mammy's bedroom to show her my new dress. I had to avoid Mrs Mallory's watchful eye in order to gain access to the bedroom where poor mammy lay ill. We children had been forbidden to go into her room, but I did so want her to see me in my new dress.

Mrs Mallory came to look after us six children whenever mammy was ill or confined. I disliked her gruff Scottish voice. She had a thick Glaswegian accent I found difficult to understand. Finally, seizing my chance, I escaped Mrs Mallory's vigilance and approached mammy's bed. She was lying, eyes closed, propped up on many pillows, her rasping breathing frightened me. She opened her eyes suddenly, seemingly aware, but then I noticed she had a far-away look as if seeing through me.

'Mam', I said softly, 'I've got my communion dress on and Pa has taken my picture.'

'That's right', she murmured, 'put it over there dear'.

'What'? I said. She didn't answer and were it not for the terrible sound of her breathing I could have supposed her dead. She had the same waxy look that Grandma Pank had when we children saw her in her coffin. I stood and watched her apprehensively. I wanted desperately for her to notice me but she had gone where I could not follow.

Mrs Mallory came into the room. 'What on earth are ye deeing in he-err?' she said angrily.

'Showing mammy my new dress'.

'Come noo, oot o' this. Yer mammy's too poorly t' be bothered wi' sich things', and she bundled me out of the room.

When I told my big sister what mammy had said, I was told she was delirious – of course I didn't really understand. That day stays in my memory as being an extraordinary one.

Receiving the 'Blessed Sacrament' for the first time I was filled with awe by the ceremony, knowing that this was the body and blood of our saviour Jesus Christ and that I must pray an extra 'special intention' prayer for my poor mammy. Surely, I thought, as I looked up at Jesus hanging there on the cross, he would help her to get rid of this strange delirious sickness. His face as he looked down on me was kind. I left the church confident that he would help our mammy to get better.

Mother continued very ill for some weeks, her condition made more precarious because of the child she carried. She came through the crisis and I learned afterward how near death she had been. The doctors gave up hope of saving the child, however against all odds he survived, though brain damaged – poor mite.

This little soul was to endure much, for at three years of age he was badly scalded by tipping over a pan of hot milk which ran down on to his face. This further retarded his speech and he did not learn to talk until he was nearly seven. Mother never ceased to blame herself for leaving the pan with the handle turned outwards. She saved the child's face from being badly scarred by pouring a full bottle of liquid paraffin over it. He was to bear the scars on his chest for the rest of his life. We were all taught to be protective of Harry and many were the fights we had in doing so. Children can be cruel and Harry's stammering nervousness was always mocked by his peers.

This strange 'day of days' stands out in my memory for another reason, my uncle had come to the house bringing with him a magical box. Father and he were fiddling with it on the table. There were ear phones attached by wires to this box. We children took turns to listen. There was the sound of a band playing. It sounded just like the band we were used to hearing in the park on our Sunday afternoon walks. We were listening for the very first time to a radio broadcast. It seemed like magic to us. Nowadays one can hardly realise there was a time before radio.

Home Cures

Mother sent me to the chemists at the onset of winter. A skinny undersized ten-year old, I skipped along to the rhythm of the words on the paper chanting them aloud like some ancient incantation.

3 pennorth of Li-cor-ice
3 pennorth of Lau-da-num
3 pennorth of An-i-seed
3 pennorth of Ch-lor-ine
3 pennorth of Pott-asium-bromide
3 pennorth of Ipe-cacu-anha.

These nice sounding words fascinated me, as did the making of the cough mixture for which these ingredients were needed. Home doctoring was mother's speciality. She would take a large pan, add water, together with a tin of black treacle, a little rum and some brown sugar, then stirring in the ingredients I had brought from the chemists, she would gently simmer it all for a while and, when cool, would pour it into bottles. This mixture would be used to treat the family's coughs and colds during the winter months.

Mother also made elderberry wine. The berries were gathered from the trees in the garden and together with my sisters I helped to pull the berries from their stalks. This wine was very soothing for sore throats and was drunk mulled at Christmas time. She once made the mistake of bottling before fermentation had finished. We awoke one night to what sounded like gun-fire coming from the cellar. The corks of two dozen bottles of wine popping-off at intervals sound tremendously loud in the quiet of the night. The white-washed walls of the cellar looked as if a blood-bath had taken place. Father teased poor mother about it for a long while afterwards. She was upset at losing most of the wine, but soon rallied to make up some more from dandelions. This wine was said to be very good for the kidneys.

Brown paper soaked in vinegar and warmed gently in the side-oven of the kitchen range was a welcome relief for earache. Small bags of salt warmed in the same way and held against the face with a scarf were used to relieve toothache. If that failed, a half tea-spoon of whisky would be given with the instruction to hold it against the offending molar until a visit to the school dental clinic could be arranged. The treatment was free for the very poor but pride in paying one's way was very important to mother, so she usually put sixpence in the box which was provided for donations.

Tooth-paste was something mother couldn't afford so we cleaned out teeth with salt. It was used for gargling also whenever anyone had a sore throat or had been near infectious diseases. I remember my best friend being taken ill with diphtheria. Having helped her home from school and been in close proximity to her, mother made me gargle several times with a strong saline solution and I was forced to swallow some which made me vomit. I didn't catch diphtheria but whether this was due to mother's ministrations or my natural immunity I can't say.

Sulphur and treacle was given regularly in the spring-time to clear the blood of impurities. We children called this 'brimstone and treacle'.

A tendency towards boils was treated with real brewer's yeast obtained from the local brewery. Stings of all kinds were treated with Reckitt's blue-bags. In these days of detergents the blue-bag is outdated, but if a housewife back then prided herself on the whiteness of her wash, a blue-bag was a must.

All spots and abrasions were treated with Witch Hazel, something I use even today. Tincture of myrrh was used to treat mouth ulcers. Boracic ointment was a good drawing agent, so was Epsom salts.

Kaolin poultice was used for bronchial problems and aspirin was the panacea for all pain relief, just as it is in various forms today.

Mentholatum was also used to help the breathing, whilst camphor was hung around the necks of school children to ward against colds. I often think the whole classroom must have smelt like a giant mothball to the poor teachers.

Goose-fat from the Christmas bird was also used for relieving congestion of the chest and other areas. For sprains and lumbago there was always the strong smelling Sloan's liniment.

Mother was nothing if not resourceful. She kept a few hens at one time. We had a ginger cockerel, a very fierce bird. The downstairs lavatory was at the bottom of the yard. If the cockerel was loose in the garden it would try to peck one's legs and had to be fended off with the sweeping brush. This made a visit to the lavatory a very hazardous affair. One day this cockerel lost the use of its legs and kept falling over. 'I think that bird has rheumatism', mother declared. She captured it by throwing a net curtain over it, and then proceeded to treat it with Sloan's liniment. This was a very fiery experience for the cockerel who squawked mightily, but ran about as normal shortly afterwards.

Mother believed in prevention rather than cure and so we were regularly dosed every night with a table-spoon of cod-liver oil which was bought loose by the quart from Boots the Chemist. As a special treat we were occasionally given Virol, which had a lovely treacle taste. All seven children were told to stand in line to receive the nightly dose of cod-liver oil. I well remember the struggle to be first in the queue so as to get a goodly squeeze of the juice from the piece of orange mother used to make the oil more palatable. She made one orange last several days!

We all had to endure the pain of the 'nit' comb on a Friday night. With head bent over a sheet of newspaper, mother would pull the fine-toothed steel comb through our hair to the accompaniment of our squeals. 'Stay still', she would command, 'I'm not having any of mine coming home with a green paper'. This referred to the practise of giving a child a green form to take home if the visiting school nurse found anyone had head lice. I never received one, but felt the shame of those who did!

Since her severe illness, when she almost died, my mother had a tendency towards bronchitis and had to cosset herself. Father bought her Scott's Emulsion. She always pulled a face when taking it for she disliked the taste. I think she also did it to show us that she too had to take unpleasant medicine.

In the nineteen twenties a visit to the doctor cost two shillings and sixpence. If he came to the house on a visit it cost five shillings, which was a lot of money when one considers the average man's wage was about two pounds ten shillings a week. Father joined a hospital scheme and paid three-pence per head for us to be covered in case we ever needed to be taken to hospital. You were charged for the ambulance I believe, except if in an accident on the road. There was no free health scheme as there is today. I am frequently amazed at how my parents coped with life and rearing seven children in those times.

If they were alive today they would no doubt think us a lot of 'molly-coddles' with our wonderful Health Service and care for the elderly. In their day if elderly folk had no one to care for them they were sent to the work-house, a severe place indeed where the bare necessities were provided and where often husband and wife were separated for the first time in their married lives.

Many men joined 'sick clubs'. I remember my father paying into one called the Odd Fellows and another rejoicing in the name of the Buffaloes. This was a prudent thing to do in case the main bread-winner was taken ill. A sick-note from the doctor to prove illness was required and this only after three days of the illness. This prevented men from taking the odd day off because they would then receive no pay either from their employer or the club. Malingerers were very much frowned upon.

In later years mother would tell of the times when father went to work even though he was ill. In the early stages of their marriage he just couldn't afford to be off work with a wife and seven children to support. During the general strike father started buying and selling furniture. It was my parents' proud boast that during this time they were able to take us all away for a week's holiday at the sea-side. He strove to do his best for us and it is only now, years later, that I can appreciate his endeavour.

Ryehill

When I was eight years old we moved to what we thought of as 'the country'. A large new housing estate had been built on the outskirts of the city in East Hull. We were given a new four-bedroom house which was lit by electricity and had a large garden.

My brothers and I were fascinated by this wonderful lighting arrangement and upon arriving at our new home dashed madly about the house switching the lights on and off until mother turned us out to explore the neighbourhood.

There was an open green play-area at the end of Ryehill Grove on which we children played ball games. Upon this green were two bench seats, which were the starting point for our favourite game of all. We called it 'Relavio'. I'm sure it is played in various forms even today.

The person who was 'it' had to seek out the ones who were hiding and race them back to the starting point. If 'it' got there first he took the other player prisoner, the other players then had to relieve him by touching the starting post without 'it' touching them.

This game would go on for hours sometimes because there were such good places in which to hide. Nearby was Sutton Drain which ran into the River Hull. It had steep grassy banks with lots of bushes and hawthorn hedges. One could hide out indefinitely here or go on until, weary of hiding, it was preferable to show oneself and enjoy the thrill of the chase.

The water was clean in Sutton Drain and men fished along its banks. We were not supposed to go into the water but about a mile up the 'river' was a sandy bottom area where boys used to swim. They called this 'bare buck' swimming. We naughty girls would sometimes creep up behind the hedge and peer at them. I too was one of the guilty though it troubled me for I never dared to mention it in confession and was convinced that I was committing that most heinous of crimes – living with a mortal sin on my soul.

The head of our school, Sister Mary Perpetua, who took us for religious instruction, would stress the dangers to our souls of 'living in mortal sin' We seemed to be in constant danger of doing this for if mass were missed on a Sunday for instance, one immediately entered this state, and if unfortunate enough to be killed or to die in some other sudden way before a 'good confession' could be made, one would go straight to Hell! No doubt existed in my mind that this would be my ultimate destination for in not confessing all my sins at the weekly Friday night confessional I frequently made what was unforgiveable – a bad confession.

This only troubled me deeply at nights when I said my prayers. Then I would pray in desperate repetition, 'Please forgive me Lord for I have sinned', promising him the while that I would not do so again but knowing in my secret heart that before the week was out I would have done so. Then for a little while I would have to be extra careful whilst crossing the road and remember to avoid walking under ladders – thus trying to avoid an early death so as to escape the flames of hell.

It was no wonder out minds were so occupied with sin and the dire consequences one might suffer indulging in same with all the religious instruction we received every day.

We had at that time an elderly Irish priest in charge of the parish. He was of the old school, preaching 'hell and brimstone' sermons to us on Sundays. Mother didn't care for him very much, especially as he spent much of his time haranguing his parishioners for the smallness of the collection.

'He shouldn't talk like that', mother declared, 'especially when he stands at the church door reeking of whisky'.

Mother crossed swords with this priest over education. My brother and I attended the Sacred Heart School. The classes were so large that even though my brother Bernard was eighteen months older than me we were both in the same class. Our teacher was an Irish lady called Miss McGlinchy, who seemed to dislike me. She appeared to favour my brother and was for ever holding me up to class ridicule, calling me a 'show off' on occasion.

I suppose I was rather extrovert. I was small and came from a large family with older brothers and sisters who were constantly putting me down. This probably made me precocious and attention seeking.

This teacher managed to sap my self-confidence and, what was worse I was under her teaching for two years. I developed a nervous tick and seemed prone to every little ailment going. I was often away from school which didn't do much for my education. Mother saw that I was not happy and finally took me away from that school and sent me to the Protestant school near my home for a while.

Father Flanagan came down to remonstrate with mother and told her she was failing in her duty. Mother lost her temper and threatened him with the frying pan she was holding at the time. He made a hasty retreat and it was some time before he called on us again. Things were smoothed out at school and I returned, albeit reluctantly. Miss McGlinchy was noticeably nicer to me for the rest of the term.

It was a different story at my next school when I came under the gentle influence of Sister Mary Joseph, our music teacher, who took an interest in me. I had a good singing voice and a knowledge of music and took part in all the annual musical competitions at the City Hall with the school choir.

I remember the last night of these competitions when the massed choirs sang in part song 'Jerusalem' and 'Rule Britannia' to a packed hall. It was a very moving experience.

I showed an aptitude for play acting and was given the part of Toad in a school production of 'Wind in The Willows'.

The following year I played the part of the wicked fairy in the operetta 'The Sleeping Beauty'. This was a star role and I wore a red ballet dress with a huge black spider embroidered in the front. My entrance was spectacular.

The scene was set for the christening of the baby princess. Everyone was on stage when suddenly the wicked fairy arrives at the party accompanied by loud chords on the piano.

'You called all the fairies from West and from East but you never called me to join in the feast', I sang loudly. Then pointing my wand at the newly christened babe I sang, 'Now this is her doom I pronounce from this hour, if ever in palace, garden or bower, her finger she pricks whilst she's spinning a thread, she shall sleep on for aye, as though she were dead'!

The chorus loudly denounced me, 'Away, away thou wicked fay. Away, away we say'!

But of course I had my wicked way as everyone knows and succeeded in disguising myself as a poor old woman, hiding out in a little used room in the palace, persuading my minions to entice the princess to the room where I was using the fatal spinning wheel.

'I'm just a poor old woman spinning thread to earn a living for my daily bread', I sang and then coaxed the unlucky girl to help me with the spinning. She pricks her finger and the rest is history!

I was a success. Even father came to see me after a preview at home. He seldom attended school functions so I was doubly thrilled.

I was asked to join the Hull Amateur Dramatic Society along with other members of the cast. This meant travelling into the city centre at night for rehearsals. Mother was always too busy to accompany me and as I was only thirteen I wasn't allowed to travel by myself. I felt very aggrieved about this at the time as I enjoyed acting so much.

The Birthday Party

It was my birthday soon and mam said I could have a party. I didn't think to ask how many friends I could invite until one week before the big day. When I was told six was the limit, I tried desperately to double this amount as I had invited at least twelve that I could remember. In vain did I plead but mam was adamant.

'You had no business inviting so many without asking me first', she said.

How could I tell six of my friends they could not come to my party after all? A greater problem still, how to choose the favoured six? Would they want to come, knowing I had hurt the feelings of the rejected ones? 'Bother birthdays', I thought, I wish they had never been invented. What was I to do?

Walking to school with my best friend Sheila I was about to confide in her when she said, 'Mam and I went shopping yesterday and we bought you a lovely present.'

'Oh, thanks', I replied, lapsing into gloomy silence. That was something else to worry about, if no one came to my party there would be no presents. What to do? What to do? My thoughts went round and round. Maybe I'd get sick by Saturday and mam would have to call the whole thing off.

But I didn't, and soon it was Friday and at the school gates the whole class seemed to be saying, 'See you at 3 o'clock tomorrow Marjorie', their eyes bright with anticipation for they had all taken to the idea of a party with delight. Children for the most part from large families, they seldom had parties of their own. The most they were allowed was to invite one friend to tea, so the enthusiasm for my party was great.

The day dawned bright and sunny, but I didn't enjoy the fact that it was my birthday. I dressed slowly and finally went down to the living room. I was greeted by mam and my brothers.

'Many happy returns', said Jack the oldest. He produced from his pocket a crumpled brown paper parcel. 'Go on open it'. Inside was a lovely sea-shell that he had found on the beach when he went on the Sunday school outing. He had kept it for many months and didn't mind parting with it now. My other brothers had clubbed together to buy me a large bar of chocolate, they knew I would share it with them of course.

My oldest sister who worked in the largest, poshest store in town had long since left for work but had left a parcel for me. The others watched as I opened it to reveal a miniature carpet sweeper, just like the one mam used. I was very surprised to get a present from mam and dad for they had little money to spare and I thought I had to choose between a present and the party. To receive a box of water paints and a painting book, something I had longed for, seemed almost too much. I nearly confessed then but was too afraid. Oh how I wished now I hadn't asked for the party.

The day dragged by. Mam asked me to help with the weekly baking. I was allowed to put the jam in the tarts using my little finger and a small spoon. Usually I enjoyed this and the peeling of the apples to make the pies. I had been shown by my older sister how to do this without breaking the peel. One then threw the peel over the left shoulder and if one was lucky it fell in the shape of a letter, this was supposed to tell the initial of the boy's name that I would eventually marry. I believed this implicitly, but couldn't bring myself to do it this time for my heart wasn't in it.

After dinner was over I went down the garden to where our Granpop neighbour was digging up potatoes. We children all looked upon this kindly old man as our grandfather, though in reality he was just a neighbour living with his daughter's family. They all called him Granpop and so did we. I often told him my troubles and thought to confide in him about the party. Maybe if he would tell mam what I had done she wouldn't lose her temper. I knew I would just die of shame if she shouted at me in front of my friends.

But Granpop was concentrating on the job in hand and said only a brief, 'Hello and how's my birthday girl?'

'Alright', I managed, unable to say more. He didn't seem to notice that I needed his full attention. No help there I thought.

I wandered back to the front gate again. Peering through the window I could see mam setting the table for tea. There was a plate of potted meat sandwiches, another of salmon paste, tarts from the morning's baking, an arrangement on a lovely china plate from the cabinet of pink and white iced biscuits, a large bowl of trifle and in the centre of the table stood a sponge cake with chocolate icing and nine little white candles on it. I looked upon the scene with a gloomy eye. Hardly enough food for six, never mind the twelve I had invited – or was it fourteen? – I couldn't remember. If I was to run away from it all where could I go? No use to think of going to a friend's house, they would all be coming here soon.

Good heavens! Here was Sheila with Mary Battey coming down the street now, too late to do anything. I would just wait at the gate until they all arrived, then take them in through the front door. Maybe mam, busy in the kitchen, wouldn't notice there were so many. Vain hope of course, the noise they all made giggling and chattering excitedly alerted my mam. She took in the situation at a glance. She opened her mouth and lifted her hand simultaneously. I cowered back. She took one look at my stricken face and stayed her impulsive anger. Long afterwards, when we were able to laugh about it, she told me I looked scared to death.

'I'll have to make some more sandwiches', she said, 'I wasn't expecting quite so many.' Then quietly to one side she said to me, 'It's a good job today is your birthday little madam. I'll have to send one of the lads for some more carnation milk to make the trifle go further. You're not to have any mind'.

I watched her face relax into something like laughter lines, and then turning to my friends I began to accept their presents. Only one bought a birthday card. That was her present. Three had bought me a handkerchief each, carefully wrapped in tissue paper. Marie had tied hers with a blue ribbon. Another gave me a book, the Girl's Annual. I could see it wasn't new but that didn't matter. Others just brought an apple or a few sweets, but best of all, my special friend Sheila gave me a beautiful broach in the shape of a butterfly. It looked as though it were made of real silver. I thought it would make a lovely present for my mam at Christmas time. I wanted her to have it because she hadn't shouted at me in front of my friends.

Still I knew I would probably 'catch it' after the party but for now I didn't care, birthday parties were such fun!

A Sea-side Outing

Rapidly the pile of sandwiches grew as my older sisters helped mother prepare the food for the family outing. Excitedly we younger children hunted in cupboards for buckets, spades, bats and balls. Father had promised us a day at the sea-side.

Mother always baked our bread. The flour came, a stone at a time, in large oatmeal coloured bags. When empty these bags were used to pack the food. There were potted beef and home-made brawn sandwiches with treacle and jam ones for afters.

From a tea-stall on the sands a large jug of tea with cups provided – on receipt of a deposit – would be bought. There were many such stalls dotted along the sands.

Our older sister was put in charge of us younger ones and we were all sent off to the station before our parents to wait there until they came. This branch line station was a half-hour's walk from our house.

Waiting around at the station was the worst part for we were eager to get to the sea-side. Our parents didn't arrive in time to catch the 9.15 am train, so we were left standing there as it pulled away.

Father, who had only himself to get ready for the day's outing, had shillied and shallied about so much that he caused us to miss the train. A great procrastinator, as far as we children were concerned, he must have decided to do some job or other before leaving the house.

It may have been that when looking up he had discovered a broken window catch on one of the windows which he couldn't possibly leave until he had either found a replacement or screwed the window down. Or perhaps the padlock on the coal-house door had been carelessly misplaced. Nothing could induce him to leave it open. A hunt for the missing padlock or for a replacement would have begun – train or no train. The house must be securely locked and bolted before he could leave it. He had a positive mania for protecting his property.

Meanwhile we children played games up and down the long cinder track leading to the side entrance of the station. At the end of this track was a stile with eight wooden steps leading directly on to the platform. One of my sisters sat at the top to prevent the younger ones going on to the platform.

We jumped, postured and climbed all over the railings and steps in our efforts to amuse ourselves during the long wait. We grew hungrier the while and our white blancoed sand-shoes grew dirtier as we ran up and down the cinder track. Every so often the tallest one amongst us stood on the top rail of the steps to peer over the fence to see if our parents could be spotted hurrying towards us. They were so late that we missed all the trains that morning and we had to eat our picnic lunch on the train.

Mother had infinite patience. I think she realised the futility of nagging father and simply did her best to keep him calm and try to help him achieve what he originally intended, which was to be on time for once. It was just circumstances and his nature that prevented him from doing so.

Hindsight shows that he was a very insecure person. I think Grandpa was much to blame for this. When my father was a child he had unfortunately been injured in an accident. Grandpa owned a horse-drawn carriage. Whilst helping to harness the horse it reared, knocking father to the ground and kicking him on the head.

He was ill for a long time apparently and the blow caused him to have very poor eyesight. This held him back in everything for he was made to feel he had to hide this defect. The few books he had he read painstakingly with a large magnifying glass. These books were encyclopaedias and books on metallurgy, the latter no doubt to do with his trade as an iron moulder. He listened avidly to the news bulletins and world affairs programmes on the wireless.

A proud man, he never asked for help and would tackle jobs by touch alone. Often as he felt for a hole in which to insert a screw or nail he would inadvertently hit his fingers with the hammer or screwdriver. A few choice epithets would be heard. Mother would say crossly, 'Now Bert, remember little pitchers have big ears.' This used to puzzle me somewhat.

Any bad language heard from us youngsters was heavily punished. We were taught to say soft expletives like 'darn it' instead of 'damn it', and 'jigger it' in lieu of 'bugger it'.

I remember an incident that father got blamed for. Mother had taken Bernard and me to start at a new school. She had my small brother Robert with her as well. He was just a toddler and learning to talk. We waited outside the Head Sister's room to be interviewed. Just as she came out of her study door my young brother escaped mother's hold and picked up the school bell which was standing on the floor near the door and shook it violently, thereby causing a few teachers to poke their heads from their classroom doors to see what was happening. Mother tried to take the bell from him but he was a strong youngster and was having fun and resisted her efforts. Finally she managed to wrench it from him whereupon he threw a tantrum and shouted 'Bugger, bugger, bugger!' Judging by the look on the Head Sister's face, one could tell she was not favourably impressed.

I overheard mother relating all this to my father later and chastising him for using 'language' in front of the little one. 'I was never so ashamed in my life', she said.

We all took father's poor sight for granted. He never solicited sympathy and therefore received none. He needed us to ignore it, regarding it as a defect in himself.

His father was not a kindly man. Although generous in giving money he gave little of himself to us or my father, seeming to favour his youngest son who became a chief engineer, but ignoring his eldest son who never achieved anything higher than tradesman.

Father was an iron moulder, who built ship's boilers. Grandpa who had achieved managerial status in ship building himself was ashamed of my father, whom he thought could have done better. Still, strangely, father idolised Grandpa and would hear nothing said against him.

Father was poor compared to the rest of his family and had the additional handicap of saddling himself with the burden of raising seven children. My parents were Roman Catholics and followed the R.C. teachings which didn't countenance the use of birth control. Mother told me many years later that the priest had told them they should live as brother and sister.

So, on the one hand they were made to feel guilty by their families for having so many children, and on the other hand by the church for trying to prevent themselves from having even more.

Mother learned to live with this. Although she was only a convert by marriage, she went to mass every Sunday and saw that we were all brought up in the faith. Father could not compromise his beliefs. He attended mass rarely and confession never. Even so he could not tolerate any of us falling away from the church. I suppose it accentuated his guilt. He remained a Catholic in name only to the end.

We all loved the little town of Withernsea. We were used to going there year after year. Grandpa Pank owned a summer bungalow there. After he died it was sold.

Our circumstances had been reduced somewhat by father's ill-health. Forced to take a lesser-paid job, he could only afford one week's holiday for us in the summer instead of the customary two. This single week was supplemented by the odd day trip.

The sea-side was vastly different to what it is today. Nearly everyone hired a tent and deck chairs. The tent was used for us to change into our swimming costumes. The proprieties had to be observed.

There were Pierrot shows on the sands with a proper stage and a piano. Folding chairs were place in rows for the audience. There was no admission charge, just a collection after the show. The performers wore Pierrot costumes which were a lot like the clowns' outfits one sees in the circus today, but the clown make-up was not used. We all loved the Pierrots.

There were sand-castle competitions and we would slave for hours trying to build the biggest and the best castle on the beach. I don't recall us ever winning anything. Father once won a voucher for ice-creams by displaying a certain newspaper on our tent. A man used to come round looking for a number on the front page and we were lucky that day, ice-cream all round.

Father was quite good on the sands for a short while. He wouldn't join in any ball games but would allow the younger members of the family to bury him in the sand. Occasionally he would paddle in the sea with us. Mostly he would tire of our company and inform mother that he was going for a stroll.

I once went with him and discovered that what he enjoyed most was looking at empty houses. On this occasion he took me to an estate agents and the man took us in his car to a new development. I was astonished, believing that we would shortly be buying one of these houses and coming to live at the sea-side. This was just another of Pa's pipe dreams, which in the end he did realise many years later when he finally bought a house in Hull.

When our week's holiday came around we either stayed with Mrs Baker, mother of the famous Kenny Baker the jazz trumpeter, or we would rent a bungalow. Mother really preferred to stay at Mrs Baker's for this nice woman would do the cooking for us if mother shopped for the food. This was quite a common arrangement in those days and was much cheaper than staying in a guest-house where the landlady provided the food.

I always seemed to be the one to go to the Co-operative store with mother to help her with the shopping. As a special treat she would buy two cream puffs and, because she could only afford two, we would sit in the park to eat them so as not to make the others envious. Mother said this was to be a secret. I understood quite well the problems she had and knew she would have bought cream puffs all round if she could have afforded it.

Childhood is such a magical time. I remember these happy days when the sun seemed to shine all the while. I can't recall that it ever rained! We didn't need much to make us happy: the sand, the pierrots, the band playing in the bandstand on the promenade and above all the sea and the attending mixture of smells: ozone, sea-weed, candy-floss and of course the fish and chip shop, where a large bag of chips could be bought for a penny, a real treat which we seldom had at home.

One holiday I remember very vividly was when I was about five or six. We went to stay on a farm in the old part of Bridlington. It was a very long way to the beach I remember. We spent most of this holiday in the fields and helping around the farm. The farmer used horses to plough his fields. Our greatest pleasure was being allowed to sit on these huge shire horses and to ride them back to the farm or to the near-by smithies when they needed to be re-shod.

We were not always well-behaved children. I still recall with fear the time my older sisters and brothers took me scrumping apples. We were merrily plundering the trees at the back of this house when a woman came out of the back door and shouted at us. We panicked and ran round to the front, but a man then came out of the front door and cut off our escape. There was a large compost heap against the tall brick wall which surrounded the orchard. My sisters, who were holding me between them, ran at this heap and scrambled to the top of the wall. They hesitated at the top for there was a six foot drop on the other side. I closed my eyes as I felt myself flying through the air. Fortunately this was just a county lane and the earth we landed on was reasonably soft. I scraped my knee badly as I fell over, but my sisters, intent on escaping, ignored my cries and dragged me along as fast as my small legs would carry me. That experience put me off going scrumping for at least five years. It took ages for us to clean ourselves up at the tap in the farmyard. The compost heap had been pretty ripe!

A catastrophe happened on this holiday. On the second day mother had taken us younger ones to the beach, leaving the older ones behind to help on the farm. Walking back afterwards my brother fell and grazed his knee badly. In order to have her hands free to attend to him mother hung her handbag on the railings surrounding the Priory church. We were in a narrow lane used as a short-cut to the old town.

Having bound-up Harry's knee with her handkerchief we continued on our way when mother stopped dead in her tracks exclaiming, 'My handbag!' and rushed back the way we had come. We ran after her. As we rounded the bend of the lane we came upon a shifty looking tramp with a sack over his shoulder. Mother's handbag had gone. Mother confronted the tramp and asked if he had seen a handbag. He denied having seen it. We didn't believe him for the lane was a long one and there was no one else in sight. There hadn't been time for anyone else to have come and gone. Mother then asked the tramp to show her what he had in his sack. He swore at us and ran off. This dreadful man took my mother's handbag which held all our holiday money, her reading glasses and our return rail tickets also. She particularly mourned the loss of her little silver sewing case with the emergency needles and threads which had belonged originally to her mother.

We were all too young to help although I remember wanting to. Poor mother was slightly built and no match for this tramp. He knew it and made good his escape. There was nothing we could do except report the thief to the police. They never recovered the handbag. A telegram was sent to father who had to take a day off work to come to Bridlington and bring us some money. When he arrived his waistcoat front was devoid of his customary gold watch and chain!

The V.I.P

My aunt came to tea alone. Alighting from the taxi she was wreathed in pale furs and carried an ugly snuffly pop-eyed Pekinese to match, so much so that at first I mistook it for an extra billow of her furbelows.

I watched as she was welcomed at the door by my parents. We children had been told to stay quietly in the front room until our visitor was settled in the dining room where the table had already been laid for tea.

She could not stay long as there was a show that evening, but no doubt she would be ready for her tea having just finished the matinee performance.

Shortly after her arrival we were called into the dining room and were re-introduced to our famous aunt whom we hardly knew. She was the well-known singer Elsie Day and was currently appearing at the Tivoli Theatre in Hull, together with her husband Rupert Hazell. They had recently returned from Australia where they had their own radio programme. Prior to that, they had completed a world tour with Harry Lauder's company. I studied her carefully as she sat at the table with us. This glamorous being was dressed in pale blue. Her eye shadow matched her dress. Her fair curly hair shone like spun gold in the late afternoon sun. Her white tapering fingers, with the long red painted nails and many sparkling rings fascinated me. She seemed like a princess in a fairy tale.

Her manner was dainty as she toyed with the food on her plate. I wondered if she knew the effect she was having upon us very ordinary children – who hardly ever saw much in the way of glamour – except on the rare occasions when mother and father were dressed in evening clothes to attend the Knights of St. Columba's annual dinner.

My aunt seemed oblivious to the watching eyes. At one point she addressed the snuffly little Pekinese, which was seated on her lap, 'Is Fifi hungry then?' she remarked, and picking up the boiled ham – that mother had provided as a suitable accompaniment to the salad – she fed it piece by piece to the wretched animal. Mother's face registered her disgust. In those days boiled ham was a special treat and we only ate it usually either at weddings or funerals. Potted beef paste and brawn were the poorer people's lot.

Father's Itchy Feet

Our family never stayed in one house more than a few years. Between the age of two and nineteen I had seven different addresses. This rolling-stone existence meant we were continuously meeting fresh people and making new friends.

When I was eleven we moved to 958 Holderness High Road. It had a large garden both back and front. There were apple, pear and plum trees at the rear, no need to go raiding other people's now we had our own. This move was a distinct step up from the council estate where we had lived since I was seven.

We all became expert at removals. Each was allocated a task. Mine was to pack the kitchen utensils, sauce pans etc., into mother's large clothes basket. Father would produce some tea chests from out of the loft where they were kept between moves and my sisters would pack the every-day pots, wrapping each plate, cup and saucer in lots of newspaper. We weren't allowed to pack china or glass, only mam did that.

We seldom had enough newspaper and my brother and I would be despatched to Aunt Belle's for more. Grandpa lived with her now and it was he who bought most of the papers. He was a racing man and bought them to study form. Grandpa would quiz us as to why we needed so many papers. We would shuffle our feet and mutter that we didn't know, for we had been told to say nothing yet about moving. But he always guessed and the word would go round the family, 'Bert's on the move again.' What mother thought of all these moves we were never told, presumably she agreed with them.

During the General Strike, when the whole of Britain's workers downed tools, father had earned a living dealing in second-hand furniture and pianos, because so many people had to sell all but essential furniture in order to get parish relief - this was conditional state aid providing one did not have any disposable assets – I suppose he picked up bargains. He needed large houses to spread the furniture around and to display it properly. People were constantly coming to view and buy. I don't remember much about this, except for one very nice green velvet lounge suite, with cabriole legs. Mother dug her heels in and refused to let it be sold even though father had been offered a good price for it. In later years mother told me that father's activities in the second-hand furniture trade paid for our annual holiday at the sea-side. Most people of our acquaintance only managed day trips.

Father's brother and sisters could never understand why he was always on the move. They all lived in the same houses each had acquired when they married. With the exception of course of Aunt Eva who, being on the stage, moved around the country, though she and her husband had a flat in London as their base. Two of my aunts, still alive and now in their eighties, live in their original homes.

As my brothers grew older they eyed the mound of coal with trepidation. It always seemed to them that as soon as the boards were in place – with only father able to reach in to fill the coal scuttle – that he would announce yet another move. Each move of course was to be our last. The coal houses were always large and contained about two tons of coal which would have to be bagged. This mania Pa had for hoarding the stuff seems to have dated back to the time of the General Strike, when coal was at a premium. He did not intend to be caught out again!

It would take father and my brothers hours to fill the sacks ready for the removal men who always protested at this unusual load. Father had to tip them heavily. He would then disappear for a time whilst we children and the removal men got on with loading the van. When he re-appeared he was minus his heavy gold watch and chain.

This was his bank. A visit to the pawnbrokers and he was solvent again.

I liked the bustle and upheaval of moving house. It always seemed an adventure, new neighbours, different church and different schools. It made life exciting, though I think it also made me a rather rootless person. Moving so often meant one lost touch with friends and life lacked continuity.

It was while we were living at 958 Holderness High Road that we heard over the wireless Mr Chamberlain, the Prime Minister, declare that we were at war with Germany.

We had during that week to queue at various places to be issued with gas-masks and ration books. I remember vividly the first time we heard the eerie sound of the air-raid warning siren. It happened in the middle of the night. Father shepherded us all into the hall. Mother and younger children were made comfortable under the stairs. The rest of us sat in the kitchen on the floor and under the table with our gas-mask cases open at the ready in case of a gas attack. Nothing happened at that time and a period followed which became known as the phoney war, because although the sirens sounded from time to time, life seemed to go on as before.

My parents decided to move again, this time further away from the dock area to 108 Faraday Street. This was a bad move. The first bombing of Hull took place in this area. A stick of five bombs was dropped, hitting houses across five streets. The first two houses in our street were demolished.

We were all in our Anderson shelter in the garden that night. These shelters were built of corrugated iron and sunk into the ground to a depth of three feet, and then the whole was surrounded with concrete.

Many lives were saved by these shelters. The sole opening was narrow and covered with heavy sacking to prevent the light from inside showing. Sandbags were piled up outside in case of blast.

My sister Eva's fiancée worked late in a factory and he would call to see her on his way home. Unfortunately for them the sirens usually went and they had to spend the time in the shelter with the rest of us. Maurice had sweaty feet, 'It's no use', mother would say, 'I can't stand the smell of your feet Maurice. You will have to sleep with them outside the opening.' She arranged the curtain of sacking and poor Maurice would try to sleep with his feet outside. Later after he and Eva were married he used to relate this story of how he nearly got his feet blown off!

We were curled up on the bunk beds listening to the drone of the bombers. Mother thought she could distinguish the sound of the German planes' engines from our own. 'Hold tight', she cried on this occasion, 'it's a chugger.' This was her own term for the German plane. She was often right. We held our breath. The explosions were absolutely tremendous. The ground heaved and we were momentarily deafened. Mother had forgotten to bring the government issue of rubber ear plugs. Maurice whipped his feet in pretty smartly! Debris was falling all around us. 'I hope that father is alright', said mother anxiously. Father was a part time fire warden in the neighbourhood and had the job of watching for any incendiary bombs which might fall and then put them out.

At last the all-clear sounded. We crept like moles into the moonlight, fully expecting that our house had been demolished. To our surprise it was still standing, the bombs had fallen several houses away. Glass and soot were everywhere, but there was no structural damage. Father came down the path to make sure we were alright.

My brother and I escaped parental watchfulness and walked the streets in dumb amazement at what we saw. Fire engines, ambulances and teams of rescue workers shoring up damaged houses. I saw into the bedroom of one house which had no wall. The bed leaned drunkenly against the wardrobe and perilously near the edge of the sloping floor. Strips of carpet dangled amongst the splintered wooden beams. Strangest of all was a man's evening suit still on the hanger, torn into ribbons and swinging from the branch of a tree in the garden. Blast did very strange things. I wondered what had happened to the occupants of the bed. We were to see many such scenes in the days that followed.

My father had us out of that area very quickly. He announced that he had found a house to rent in the North of the city on the outskirts. 'It will be a lot safer', he said, 'The Gerries are plastering this area because it's near the East Docks.'

We moved within three days of him finding this house. Never in all the moves we made did we pack so swiftly. Mother protested vehemently that it couldn't be done. Father was adamant and started in on the coal! He and the boys worked far into the night.

My sisters and I were despatched to the new house via two bus routes carrying brooms, buckets and cleaning materials. The house had been empty for some time and was pretty dirty. For the next three days we worked like demons, taking French leave from our jobs. Eva, Edith and I all worked at Hammonds large department store. We felt justified in absenting ourselves because the urge to find safety was strong in us.

Mother had used influence to help us get these jobs at Hammonds. She had two nieces and a nephew who held good positions there. My cousin John was head of a department and his sisters, Trudy and Gladys were buyers. It was through their help that we girls obtained employment. Jobs were at a premium at that time, which was just before the war - in the case of my sisters – I joined the firm later.

To get work in such a prestigious store as Hammonds was not easy. When our cousins first started work there they had to tie themselves to a specific time of apprenticeship and to sign debentures. Their parents had to pay the firm a premium for the privilege of their being trained. This practice had stopped by the time we three girls started work.

Our new home was at the back of Hull University, second house from the end of a long row, bounded by playing fields at the back and facing the university grounds. It was a fairly quiet area at first, but then the mobile gun units moved in! The sound of the ack-ack guns during air raids was almost as bad as the noise of falling bombs.

Often we were caught coming home along Inglemire Lane when the sirens sounded. We would hear the count-down of the gunners begin and we would run like the wind to get inside our shelter before the guns fired. As usual we would have forgotten to bring our ear plugs, these were uncomfortable, being made of hard rubber in those far-off days before plastic was invented.

Behind our house was the Corporation playing field in which was a larger shelter manned by the Fire Fighting Department. My father and brothers did their turn at fire watching and soon we had a large collection of burnt-out incendiary bombs. My brothers enjoyed spotting these devices and tackling them with sandbags before they could set the buildings on fire, thereby lighting up the whole area and making it easier for the German bombers to hit their targets.

Shortly after we moved to this house I became friendly with the girl next door. We were the same age and I liked her at once. Her name was Eileen Gilroy and like us they were a catholic family. Eileen and I used to go to church together.

She introduced me to the works of P.G. Wodehouse. We loved his books and got them out of the small lending library on Cottingham Road. This was just a book shop with a lending section and for two old pennies you could borrow a book for a week. We spent most of our Saturday afternoons in there, reading as much as we could without paying, though of course we were always obliged to take a book out in the end. We had private jokes involving Wodehouse language. It crept into our own and we talked about having a 'goodish' bit of money and 'Faugh!' became our own cry of disgust. 'He looked like a dying newt', was the most derogatory thing we could say. We 'toddled' along and cried 'toodle-pip old bean' when we said cheerio. It was all great fun.

I was working now as an apprentice milliner in Hammonds large department store. Miss Peck the head milliner was extremely strict, I longed to get past the stage of stitching velvet linings and feathers into hats, and the constant picking up of pins.

Model hats were made in this workroom for the wealthy ladies in the city. I think mother would have liked to have been a milliner, all her life she made her own hats and trimmed them in a tasteful manner. She couldn't understand why I found the work boring and why I was not too disappointed when the store was flattened one night in a particularly heavy raid.

I went to work then in a small sweets and grocery shop near my home. I could walk to work, saving money on bus fares.

Before moving from Faraday Street I had attended night school, learning short-hand and typing. I had passed my first exam but it became almost impossible to continue because the air-raid warning would sound almost every night and if I had not yet left home, mother would not allow me to go. If I reached the school before the air raid warning siren sounded, we simply spent most of the time in the shelter. No one seemed to care much about our education. I think also we lost the ability to concentrate on studying because of lack of sleep. We spent many nights in the shelter and with so much coming and going; any sleep one could snatch was always broken.

My sister Eva had a very narrow escape one day. She was cycling home for lunch from the Green Circle Library where she worked. She had to cross the railway line down Cranbrook Avenue. Usually the gate would close against her just as she got there. This day she was very fortunate in just getting through the gates and a few hundred yards down the road before a bomb dropped. We surmised later that the German plane had been trying to hit the train. She was blown from her bicycle into a ditch but wasn't seriously hurt. She arrived home white and shaking having narrowly escaped death.

Soon the coal house was nearly full again. Father - a far-seeing man in some ways – deduced that there would be more heavy bombing, so he imparted the news one day, after Eva's narrow escape, that we would all be moving to Hornsea on the coast, twenty miles away. We younger members of the family were delighted, to live at the sea-side sounded great.

We joined in the move this time with great enthusiasm. I managed to ride with mother and my two younger brothers up front in the driver's cab of the removal van. Father disappeared once again to pawn his gold watch and chain. He and the rest of the family were to catch the train.

We made this move in the spring. Later on that year double summer-time was introduced. This made it more difficult for the German bombers, because with extended daylight hours they had to face fiercer flak from the ground gunnery batteries who could see them clearly.

That first night in Hornsea Bernard and I went for a look around the amusement arcade and took a turn on the roller skating rink. Coming back along the promenade in the dark we were startled by a voice shouting, 'Halt, who goes there?'

'Us', we shouted in unison. Then Bernard gathering his wits said, 'Friend.'

'Advance and be recognised'.

We did so somewhat warily for the two soldiers with their rifles pointing at us looked very intimidating. We were made to produce our identity cards. We had to carry this card everywhere together with our gas masks. The latter was like having a box camera slung around your neck all the time. We dared not go out without our masks for we were very afraid of gas attacks. Uncle Herbert, a First World War veteran had been gassed whilst in the trenches in France and he still suffered with his chest because of it.

Hornsea was a garrison town. Thousands of troops were in and around the surrounding villages and holiday camp sites. On Sundays we became accustomed to seeing row upon row of khaki clad soldiers filling the church pews at mass. At weekends hundreds of them would use the area of beach open to the public, to play bingo, though then it was called housey-housey. Local girls, older than I, would mingle with the soldiers. Cards would be brought and pebbles on the beach used as counters.

We lived five minutes' walk away from the sea. It was a while before we became accustomed to hearing the waves breaking on the shore, particularly at night when all was quiet, except when there was a bombing raid on. I would lie awake hearing the heavy drone of the bombers from the near-by aerodromes pulsing their way across to enemy territory and would mentally wish them good luck and a safe return. How brave these flight crews were, going into battle on a daily basis, never knowing whether they would be alive tomorrow.

One week-day I was about to go swimming in the sea with a friend. Suddenly we were bundled aside by two soldiers running up the steps from the sands. 'Down, down', they shouted. Quickly we crouched behind the sea-wall.

'What is it?' I gasped.

'Keep your head down and cover your ears', said the soldier, 'there is a mine bumping against the breakwater.' This breakwater was about two hundred yards off.

We all held our breath. Nothing happened. One of the soldiers peered bravely over the wall. The mine had floated clear and was bobbing further off in the sea. We left the scene hurriedly. The soldiers went to report to the bomb squad. Later in the day the mine was exploded well away from the shore.

I was now out of work having left Hull and given up my job. Mother had a much larger house to look after. 'Inchmona' in Clifford Street had six bedrooms. She needed my help she said. In those days we teenagers had little say. So used were we to obeying our parents we hardly thought of rebelling. I stayed at home that year and hated every minute of it, particularly after the terrible blitzing of Hull when hordes of bombed-out relatives descended on us.

Independence

Barely two years had passed since the first breath of war touched us in the shape of Uncle Harry's brother arriving home from the aborted landing in France, yet much had happened. I was sixteen now and struggling for independence from my mother, so I got a job in Todd's High Class Grocery and Confectioners store in Newbegin, Hornsea.

There were seven on the staff. Mousey Piers, a lady of mature years, was in charge. Her appearance was very mouse like, small and plump, with brown hair greying a little at the temples and which she wore cut short like a man. Her sharp pointed features, narrow deep set eyes and prominent moustache accentuated her mousey appearance. Of course we younger ones were always careful to call her Miss Piers to her face, referring to her as Mousey only behind her back.

She taught me how to weigh up the rations. I would take a wire to a huge cheese which had already been skinned by the manager and cut until I had weighed up hundreds of two ounce pieces and wrapped them all in grease-proof paper. Two ounces was the weekly ration for each person. The following day I had to start on the butter. Again the ration was two ounces. Cooking fat was only one ounce each. We were allowed four ounces of margarine, four of sugar and two of tea. Even bread and cakes were rationed eventually.

The most popular thing we sold was the ham and egg pies. These were not rationed and were made by Fred Beasley and Bill Tindal in the bakery at the back of the shop. Every scrap of bacon and ham would be saved from the slicing machine. Such pieces, together with the dried egg, which came from America under the lease-lend agreements, were made into delicious pies. There was always a queue for these outside the shop on pie days.

Mr Todd, who owned the store, was a vitriolic character. He was past the age of retirement, but kept the business going for the sake of his son who was in the army. A man of great charm and distinguished good looks, his hair was silver and his features aristocratic, but he lacked patience. Occasionally his temper would erupt, especially if he had to serve at the counter during staff lunch breaks, which was often the busiest time of the day.

He soon became flustered if he had an awkward customer. All the professional and business men's wives living in Hornsea and surrounding villages were registered for rations with us. Used to having plenty, some of them took very badly to rationing and they showed it.

He particularly disliked serving Mrs Finch, a dentist's wife. Her numerous sons always seemed to be on leave and she would be demanding eggs on their emergency coupons. They were entitled of course, but the Ministry of Food was hopeless at honouring the emergency egg coupons. To supply these meant regular customers were deprived of their allotted one egg per week. What a storm this could cause.

Mr Todd not wishing to offend his customers would try to explain, but these ladies were used to having the best and would not listen. Finally in exasperation he would shout, 'Don't you know there is a war on madam, what do you expect?'

'An egg!' the irate customer would retort.

Whereupon Mr Todd would call one of us to serve the customer and muttering loudly about this 'Bloody war', he would go into his little office and slam the door. Often he would disappear for hours after one of these outbursts.

He had a wife whom he hardly ever saw. He also had a lady friend who would come after the shop was closed and help him with the book-keeping. She spotted my potential in this department and I was soon staying behind learning the mysteries of double-entry book-keeping. That was an eye-opener also, for it was the wealthiest in the town who carried the most credit.

Amongst our customers was Mrs Fanny Rix, mother of the famous Brian and Sheila. I joined the local drama group and was once in a play with Brian Rix. It was called 'Night Must Fall'. He played the part of the servant who murdered his employers. I was very small beer, playing the part of the maid. Brian had not found his talent for farce then as he did in later years, I thought he hammed his part up rather.

I made friends with Mavis Reed who also worked at Todd's. Through her I became acquainted with many of the local girls. Mavis and her friends all attended chapel. I began to question my own religion at this time and was persuaded to join a study circle held at the Methodist minister's house every Sunday evening. We enjoyed this mainly I suspect because we met RAF boys who also went there. It was all very innocent; we never went out with any of them.

Father went back to work in an engineering firm and had to travel to Hull daily. He left home very early, cycling to the station to catch the six fifteen, often not coming home until nine at night.

Mother made the most of this new-found freedom, as did I. She joined the ladies choir and became their choir mistress. Our front room was taken over for choir practice and mother was also much in demand for playing the piano at Mrs Rix's American tea dances.

In the past, father had never agreed to her playing anywhere for money. If she managed to do so she would spend the money on frivolous things. We children were exhorted not to tell father about these treats. She would take us to Fields café when we lived in Hull and we would tuck into luscious fresh cream cakes, something so different from our every-day home-baked fare.

I think she enjoyed watching us tucking in and probably felt good at thwarting father's wishes. We all knew why she didn't stand up to father. He was a typical Victorian husband and father and expected us all to obey him. He would wear one down with his persistent arguments. Mother was a natural peace-lover and couldn't stand rows, but now there came the war and father worked long hours on war work, leaving us to enjoy more freedom.

Mother and I attended the military band concerts every week at the Floral Hall. One unforgettable evening came about through my sister Edith. She was home on leave and had met one of the bandsmen in the regimental band of the Welsh Fusiliers regiment. She invited him and the conductor of the band home for a musical evening. When the band-master, who was a brilliant violinist, found that my mother could accompany him on the piano, we had a wonderful evening of first-class entertainment. Mother really came into her own and played 'Zampa' and 'Poet and Peasant' to accompany the young bandsman on the cornet. To round off the entertainment the band-master played a tune on his violin, making it sound just like the bag-pipes.

First Love

It was during this year when I was almost seventeen that I met Ronnie Pound and we fell in love.

We met through my brothers. Always dare-devils they had bet some of their friends that they could stay in the sea longer than any of them. It was the middle of winter and very cold. I went with friends on to the promenade to watch this event.

Ronnie was one of the swimmers. A six foot two Adonis, keen on body building he looked very fit. I thought him very handsome with his black curly hair and twinkling brown eyes. He had a marvellous sense of humour I was to find and we had such good times together.

He was an accomplished guitarist and accordionist. His sister also played the accordion and the piano. Musical evenings in their little cottage were a delight. His mother, a widow for some years, idolised Ronnie. He was the youngest of her nine children and should have been spoilt, but he was a very caring and generous hearted young man and I loved him dearly. He got his sense of humour from his mother who was a great leg-puller and teased us unmercifully.

I always had Sunday dinner at their house. She would pile my plate with green vegetables, then pretending not to notice that I didn't like them would ask me to have some more. Out of politeness I would eat sprouts, cabbage, etc. that I never ate at home and strangely enough I got used to them and even got to like them after a while. She became a second mother to me.

The following year Ronnie was called up into the Royal Naval Signal Corp. We wrote every day. His first leave came at last. He looked so handsome in his sailor's uniform. I fell in love more deeply than before.

In no time at all he was home again on embarkation leave. So was my brother Bernard who was in the army and cousin Herbert who flew in RAF bombers. We went around together for much of the time.

We hired rowing boats on Hornsea Mere and raced each other up and down the long stretch of water. We swam in the sea and played beach cricket.

Evenings were spent in Ronnie's mother's cottage, listening to him play the guitar and also to him and his sister Norah playing accordion duets.

I shall never forget those romantic moonlight walks as he escorted me home after the dances at the Floral Hall. Time seemed to stand still for a little allowing us young things to be as nature intended, care-free and playful. Except that the underlying fear was in all our minds but we did our best to ignore it.

My cousin was particularly brave. He knew the odds against his survival were poor. He was a rear-gunner in Wellington bombers. These poor devils were despatched nightly.

We were on the beach one day running towards the sea. Herbert tripped over a stone and sat nursing his twisted ankle. I helped him up. 'Have you sprained it?' I asked.

'Only slightly, I wish to God I'd broken it', he added ruefully. Then seeing my expression added, 'Forget it kiddo, I didn't mean it.'

But we both new a 'blighty wound' would have grounded him for a while, giving him a better chance of survival. His plane was lost shortly afterwards in a raid over Mannerheim.

The end came all too quickly; Ronnie's ten days leave was over. I went with him to the bus stop. On impulse he asked me to ride through to Hull with him. We knew this was the last bus and I would have to remain on it in order to come straight back for it simply turned round at the Hull bus station and returned to Hornsea.

His mother and sister were standing at the lane end as we passed in the bus. They waved and his mother was crying. We didn't talk much, just held hands, so very young and so in love. Before we reached the terminus Ronnie asked me to wait for him and not go out with anyone else. I agreed to do so. We promised to write every day. He kissed me and then I was alone on the top deck of the bus.

I was glad it was dark for the return journey. I cried most of the way home. It was so hard at seventeen to be in love and know that the man one loved was going off to fight a war. I had the most terrible foreboding that he wouldn't come back.

Some weeks later he was killed in the landing at Algiers in North Africa. His sister came into the shop with the telegram in her hand. I was devastated and had to go home.

It was strange to realise that Ronnie had already been dead for three days before we heard about it, for I had felt him very near to me, he even made me laugh. If that sounds fanciful I can't help it for I believe the soul stays earth bound for a little time until our grief blots them out and sends them on their journey. He was so young, so full of life. I couldn't believe he was gone.

Despairingly I tried to get away by joining the land-army. Being not quite seventeen and a half I needed my parents' consent. They wisely wouldn't give it. My mother was very understanding and allowed me to spend all my spare time at Mrs Pound's cottage.

I think we three women helped each other. Norah and her mother took me everywhere with them. We visited other members of their family still living in Hull and we went to the local cinema together and Norah and I would walk miles on Sundays.

Norah was much older than me and had been married but was separated from her husband. Then she met Johnny a warrant officer in the RAF. He became a frequent visitor to the cottage and gradually Norah started playing the accordion again for him and I played the piano. After the war she divorced her husband and married Johnny. We kept in touch for many years.

We played card games and Mrs P, as I called her, started to laugh and regain her sense of humour. Gradually the intense pain of losing Ronnie began to diminish for me. I was young and resilient and after eighteen months or so I started to go to dances again.

Both my older brothers were now overseas. Jack was in the big push towards Paris. Bernard was in Burma fighting the Japanese. He poor lad had a tough time but was spared to come back to us. He went away a boy and came back after four years, a man.

Mother like countless others exhorted us to pray for their safety. I could hardly do so, for I had asked God to keep Ronnie safe and he hadn't listened. My faith was practically non-existent at this time.

Sister Edith was in the WRNS stationed at Millhill in London and subject to the buzz bombs, with which London was being bombarded. These were pilotless rocket bombs. She told me how terrifying it was listening for the engine to cut out. Her nerves were pretty shattered when she came home on sick leave. Fortunately she managed a change of posting and worked in the mail office at Lowestoft until she was demobbed.

Our town was now full of the Free French Army. I saw General de Gaulle pass through the town one day on his way to inspect his troops at Rolston. Very tall and upright, he looked a match for any German. We waiting crowds cheered him mightily as he passed in his armoured car. He ignored us entirely.

It was fun at the dances meeting the French boys. We girls thought they were very naughty and fast. No sooner would they have asked you to dance than they would say, 'You sleep with me tonight …yes?' The answer was always a very firm 'No!' At the same time we were aware of girls who did.

As each battalion moved out there was always a rear guard left behind to clear up. Dances were pretty bleak and there would be hardly any partners.

The virgins danced together – some married ladies and the 'tarty' dames always managed to get the male partners. This was very noticeable when the advance parties arrived. My friends and I figured that the departing regiments left telephone numbers and addresses on the barrack room walls.

Still, apart from lacking partners we didn't wish to emulate these others. It was very different then. There was no 'pill' and it was just accepted that nice girls waited until they were married or were at least engaged before indulging in sex. I believe most men expected to marry a virgin. Also the risk of having an illegitimate child was so frightening. It happened to a girl called Francis that I knew. She tried to commit suicide; the stigma and shame were so enormous. There was of course no state aid; the girl's parents had to keep the child.

I was turned eighteen now and had to register. I wished to join the ATS but was told that the forces intake was closed and only work or other essential jobs were on the agenda. I was asked to work in an ammunition factory in Leeds.

Both my older sisters had worked as 'clippies' on the East Yorkshire buses at one time. This was considered essential work as it released a male bus conductor for the forces. Mother persuaded me to do this. At least, she said, I'd be one less for her to worry about. The war was very hard on mothers; they lived in a perpetual state of anxiety, dreading the sight of a telegraph boy with bad news from the war office.

Clippie

At the age of eighteen I was called upon to do essential war work. The forces were closed to assimilate the previous draft, so there were only two options open to me. I could work on munitions or be a bus conductress. My mother persuaded me to do the latter as she wanted me to stay at home.

I worked out of Hornsea depot for the East Yorkshire Bus Company which ran long distance buses between towns. I found this interesting at first. We worked split shifts so that one could find oneself with a stop-over of one or two hours in another town before making the return journey.

I used to spend such time looking round the shops, museums, etc. If the stop-over was in the middle of the day I went to the workers' orchestral concerts at the City Hall. One could wander in and out at will and people would sit and eat lunch while listening to the music. This was infinitely preferable to sitting in the bus depot canteen.

In Beverley I made frequent visits to the Minster. One day I joined a party of school children who were being shown around by the verger. I lost track of the time. When I realised how late it was I hurried to the Market Place only to discover that my bus had gone without me.

The driver had to keep to his schedule. He had collected some fares but could not issue tickets. Finally he drove to the Beverley depot and they provided him with a spare conductor. I had the ignominy of travelling back to Hornsea on the next service bus as a passenger.

The depot manager reported me of course and I was called into the General Manager's office in Hull. I wanted 'out' and told him so. He informed me that as the job was classified as essential war work I could not leave. He suspended me for three days and in addition I lost two days' pay. There was nothing I could do about it.

Hornsea was a garrison town and I had some rude awakenings dealing with the military. There were army and air-force bases all around that area. Off-duty soldiers and airmen were reasonable passengers when coming into town; it was a different story after the pubs emptied.

There were ribald remarks and some would try to 'chat me up', patting me on the bottom the while. Once I was actually 'goosed' by an amorous French soldier. I hated this familiarity and always showed them a frozen demeanour. Some of the things that happened though were quite funny in retrospect. Such an occasion arose when we were on our way from Hessle to Beverley one evening.

We stopped outside the barracks on the outskirts of the town. The waiting horde of soldiers rushed on to the bus. I protested that there were too many of them. A strapping sergeant pulled me on to his knee and held me there while another rang the bell for the bus to proceed.

I finally freed myself and endeavoured to collect the fares. This was difficult as there were so many standing. When I finally arrived on the top deck I was horrified to find it absolutely full and about fourteen men standing up. This was against all regulations and very dangerous. I rang four bells for the emergency stop.

My driver was all of four foot ten inches tall. He was thin and wiry and wore glasses; it was difficult to imagine a more inoffensive looking man. His name was Tommy Carr. He got out of the driver's cab and came round to confront the army.

'This bus goes no further until some of you get off', he said in his most authoritative manner. Then as none of the army lads moved, 'Come on lads, I'm sorry about it, but I could lose my license if I break the law'.

Still no one moved. Then Tommy, standing his ground, took out his pipe and tobacco pouch and proceeded to fill his pipe, making it plain he wasn't going to give in.

Then the sergeant spoke, 'OK, all those standing on the top deck – Off!' They did so, albeit reluctantly. I told Tommy afterwards that I admired his stand. He said that he knew something was wrong as soon as he went round the first bend for the bus swayed so much he could hardly keep control.

On another late shift one of the drunks on the top deck urinated out of a window. I simply didn't go up to collect fares. I was boarded by the Inspector who reported me and again I had to see the Depot Manager. I complained about doing this shift and told him I refused to do it in future. We had only one male conductor who was elderly but a good sport. He took over that Rolston bus route whenever it was possible for him to do so. I never did that run again.

It was very tiring standing on these long journeys. If I was on at night there was the additional problem of trying to see to punch the correct amounts on the tickets. Because of the blackout we wore a bicycle lamp around our necks in order to see. Batteries were scarce and lamps often had little power. Also the interior lights of the bus were blacked-out except for a tiny bit at the bottom which emitted only a very dim light.

We were always pleased if we managed to get beyond the city boundaries without the sirens blowing. If an air-raid occurred we had to stop the bus at the nearest street shelter and see to the safety of the passengers. If we were out of the city we were allowed to continue.

On country roads we frequently lost our bearings. The driver would stop the bus and I would have to enlist the aid of a passenger and reconnoitre to find our whereabouts. At some of the smaller places the bus didn't go through the village but merely stopped at the lane ends. These were easily missed in the dark.

Foggy wintery evenings were a nightmare. In those days all the double-decker buses were open. It was cold and draughty standing on the platform and the journey in the dark seemed interminable. I had to concentrate though in order to keep track of the route and help the passengers to get off at the right stop.

In 1944 there was talk of the war ending soon. I was aware that I had to get some training if I was to better myself. There were no night classes in Hornsea so I enrolled at the Greg Business College in Hull. My father paid the first twenty pounds and I had to find the rest myself.

Things were made doubly difficult by my having to work shifts. I would try to swop as often as I could so as to finish early and get through to Hull for my evening class. In this way I progressed.

I had a friend, Phyllis Moxley, who worked in an insurance office. She managed to smuggle me into her office occasionally when she was working overtime. I would practise my typing on the office machine. So it was in this hit-and-miss fashion that I acquired a knowledge of office routine and was eventually able to get a job in an accountant's office in Hull.

Talk about burning the candle at both ends! I certainly did, with disastrous results on at least one occasion. Often after college I would go to a late dance at the Floral Hall, not getting to bed until the early hours of the morning. This lack of sleep caused me to have a humiliating experience which in retrospect sounds funny but at the time was rather embarrassing.

I sometimes had to work a 'spare shift'. I had to report to the depot at 5.45 am in case any conductress missed their shift. The first bus left at 6.05 am. I must have been very tired to sleep through the alarm. I was rudely awakened by my mother rushing into the bedroom crying, 'Marjorie, wake up, there is a bus full of passengers outside the front door.'

Springing out of bed I peeped through the curtains and was horrified to meet the gaze of workmen sitting on the top deck of the bus looking very put out indeed.

I dressed as quickly as I could, not for the first time cursing the uniform, which was made in the siren suit fashion, the top being attached to the trousers, there were buttons everywhere. A most complicated garment to don, I knew it could only have been designed by a man!

Shortage of hair curlers to curl one's hair while sleeping meant that we were reduced to using pipe-cleaners. These instruments of torture were impossible to unwind with any speed without giving oneself a few bald patches. I tried without success and finished up having to wind a scarf around my head, turban fashion. In my haste the only scarf I could find was far too large for this. As I glanced in the mirror I saw that I looked like a demented version of Carmen Miranda or the Maharaja of Shangapour.

There was no time to do anything about it as the driver of the bus, one Henry Banks, an impatient type with whom I had crossed swords on more than one occasion, was sounding his horn at frequent intervals shattering the peace of the sleeping neighbours, who were beginning to peer out from windows to see what all the noise and fuss was about.

Furthermore he kept the engine running making more noise than he need. The whole street was agog by the time I emerged sheepishly to take charge of the bus.

The passengers, nearly all male, regarded me with astonishment as I proceeded to unwind my head-dress and remove the pipe-cleaners, one by tortured one. I had briefly debated with myself whether to keep the turban on until I arrived at the Hull depot, thereby enlarging the amount of ridicule I would have to endure. I chose to remove it as the lesser of two evils, besides which the prospect of trying to keep the turban on my head during the jolting and jerking of the journey would be nigh impossible.

Henry Banks was a demented driver, how he ever managed to get a licence to drive public transport was a mystery. He was so bad that elderly passengers upon seeing who was driving would say, 'No thank you dear, I'll catch the next one.'

Henry was six foot five in his stocking feet as he was fond of telling us. The driver's cab was far too small for him; he crouched there like a malevolent spider, looking terribly uncomfortable. Whether this contributed to his impatient bad temper I don't know. He had a habit of rushing towards a bus stop as though not intending to halt then standing on his brakes at the last moment. This made everyone, particularly the conductress who was standing, be precipitously propelled down the aisle. We girls hated being on shift with him, we called him 'Mad Henry'.

He almost caused me to have a nasty accident one day. We were returning from Hessle, which was a two hour journey. The run had been hectic through the villages, people getting on and off all the while and we were running late. Henry, determined to make up time drove very fast. As he swung round a sharp corner I was coming down the stairs and was pitched forward only just managing to save myself from being hurled into the road by grabbing the outer rail on the platform. My money bag, which was very full, swung out spilling the money over the tail board into the road. I rang four bells for an emergency stop. Henry pulled up. It took us a while with the help of one or two passengers to find my takings. At the end of the week I was over thirty shillings short and had to pay it myself. Henry denied any blame; he was not exactly my favourite person!

At last came VE Day in 1945. A roar went up from the assembled crowd on the cliff-top at Hornsea as the huge bonfire took hold and after six bleak years of darkness, light was re-born. The faces of the people in the flickering light of the dancing flames shone with almost primeval delight. I felt as early man must have done when he first discovered fire.

People were deliriously happy. At last the six long weary years of war were over. Germany had capitulated and the war in Europe was at an end. Church bells rang joyfully, their peels no longer a warning of invading enemy troops, but a sound of freedom as expressive as the glow of the enormous bonfire lighting up the night sky, heralding the peace.

To be young at such a time and to have experienced the euphoria we felt at the coming of that peace is something that almost beggars description. We danced and sang the whole night through. The older people drifted away until there was just a nucleus of young ones. An impromptu band appeared, an accordionist and a guy with a tin whistle, who also played the mouth organ.

Tiring, we sat on the grass and joined in the singing. 'Bless 'em all', I chorused, then felt the sudden sting of tears as the words struck home and I remembered my first love, Ronnie Pound, killed at Algiers, Colour Sergeant Harry Bates, another boyfriend, lost in the Normandy landings, George, an air-force navigator with whom I'd had a brief friendship, and my cousin Herbert, lost over Mannerheim in a bombing raid, together with countless others who had died so young. They had given their lives so that we might live in freedom.